Letter to General Franco

Fernando Arrabal

translated and annotated by
Peter Thompson

with a preface by
Phyllis Zatlin

epilogue by
Francisco González Viera

and a coda by
Miguel Hernández

DIÁLOGOS
NEW ORLEANS
DIALOGOSBOOKS.COM

Letter to General Franco
Fernando Arrabal
Translated by Peter Thompson

Copyright © 2025 by Fernando Arrabal, Peter Thompson and Diálogos Books..

All rights reserved. No part of this work may be reproduced in any form without the express written permission of the copyright holders.

Printed in the U.S.A.
First Printing

Book design: Bill Lavender
Cover photo is a Francoist demonstration in Salamanca in 1937, after the capture of Gijon. Wikimedia commons, public domain.

Publisher's Cataloging-in-Publication Data
Names: Arrabal, Fernando, author. | Thompson, Peter, translator.
Title: Letter to General Franco / Fernando Arrabal ; translated by Peter Thompson.
Other titles: Carta al general Franco. English.
Description: New Orleans, LA : Diálogos, 2025. | Summary: Arrabal, whose father was imprisoned by the Franco regime, sends an open letter begging Franco to stop the regime's cruel treatment of political prisoners.
Identifiers: LCCN 2024950715 | ISBN 9781956921373 (pbk.)
Subjects: LCSH: Franco, Francisco, 1892-1975. | Fascism – Spain – 20th century. | Political prisoners – Spain. | Political persecution – Spain – History – 20th century. | Spain – Politics and government – 1939-1975. | BISAC: HISTORY / Europe / Spain. | POLITICAL SCIENCE / Political Ideologies / Fascism & Totalitarianism.
Classification: LCC DP269.63 A77 2025 | DDC 946.081--dc23
LC record available at https://lccn.loc.gov/2024950715

ISBN 978-1-956921-43-4 (pbk)

DIÁLOGOS
NEW ORLEANS
DIALOGOSBOOKS.COM

Acknowledgments

The translator warmly thanks Fernando Arrabal for his humor, iconoclastic vigor, surrealism and his many plays—among the most often produced in the world. And for his kindness and generosity toward this translation.

We are immensely grateful to Professor Phyllis Zatlin for her knowledge of Arrabal's Spain, her remembrance of the Franco years, and her personal connection to Arrabal.

Everyone involved in this translation has thought soberly—*acknowledgment*, here, takes on its suggestion of *consciousness*—of Macario, whose letter from jail ends Arrabal's *Letter*. The same is true of Miguel Hernández (coda to the translation), of his family, and of the tens of thousands who suffered reprisals *after* the Civil War.

The translation of Hernández's poem is my own.

Contents

Preface	7
Letter to General Franco	17
Epilogue	103
Coda: Lullabies of the Onion	105

Preface

Are there people today who really admire dictators and want to have them in control? Now is the time for all of us to revisit philosopher George Santayana's wisdom: "Those who cannot remember the past are condemned to repeat it."

Fernando Arrabal (b. 1932) has never forgotten the past. Throughout his life he has repeatedly and eloquently called attention to the evils in his native Spain of the Franco regime (1939-1975). This first translation provides readers of English the opportunity to consider his powerful letter to Francisco Franco, written before that dictator's death but unfortunately relevant to contemporary circumstances in many countries, not excluding the United States.

I discovered Arrabal after joining the faculty of Rutgers University's Department of Romance Languages. With my colleagues in French, we were teaching an anthology that featured works by important new voices in France, among them Arrabal's quasi autobiographical first novel, *Baal Babylone*. I informed my associates that Arrabal was Spanish; they assured me that he was French. After all, Germaine Brée had chosen him for her prestigious textbook and he wrote in French. Obviously I was wrong.

Of course it was those young men who were wrong. Not only was Arrabal Spanish but Spanish literature has well-known antecedents for his own character of formidable, hypocritical, tyrannical mothers (as in the novel mentioned), including Benito Pérez Galdos's novel *Doña Perfecta* (1876) and Federico García Lorca's play *The House of Bernarda Alba* (*La Casa de Bernarda Alba,* 1936; premiere in Buenos Aires, 1945). Despite the tradition of conservative mothers, often conspiring with the Church in opposing men of liberal ideas—even if that meant arranging a murder—Arrabal was not following literary tradition in his creation of a mother image but rather was reacting to the disappearance of his father. It should be noted in passing that García Lorca, already world famous as poet and playwright, was assassinated at the beginning of the Civil War and his works were prohibited in Spain for years thereafter.

Lieutenant Arrabal refused in July 1936 to join the Francoist military coup against the duly-elected Republican government and was subsequently erased from family history. A little boy mourned his father whom he never saw again. As he grew up, Arrabal searched for his father and blamed his mother. By the time he wrote his monologue *Carta de amor (como un suplicio chino)* (premiere March 27, 2001), he had made peace with her and understood how women, too, had been victimized by the terrible circumstances that in this "love letter" he labels a Chinese torture. His letter to Franco comes long after those circumstances occurred, but they inform us of what can happen when we are not politically alert.

Finding historical accounts of the aftermath of the Spanish Civil War (1936-39) is no longer difficult. No one should welcome a bloodbath, think that a war can be ended quickly, or believe that once there is a cease-fire all will go back to normal. In *Las bicicletas son para el verano* (1982), a boy wants a bicycle for the summer of 1936. As Don Luis makes clear to his son Luis in 1939, the long siege of Madrid at war's end brought no peace, only victory. The father in the play by Fernando Fernán Gómez (1921-2007) had not fought in the war but will be purged, probably sent to a concentration camp, and will not be allowed to work. The boy will have to support the family.

Twentieth century Spanish history reveals that suppression and intentional misinformation can continue for generations and that victors tend to wipe out progress made by their predecessors. During and immediately following the armed conflict, many people were killed, imprisoned, went into hiding, fled the country temporarily or self-exiled for years. Spain lost numerous intellectuals, creative artists, and theater practitioners, along with average citizens who yearned to be free or could not find work at home. The diaspora included works of art. Pablo Picasso (1881-1973) would not allow his masterful anti-war painting *Guernica* (1937) to go to his native Spain until after Franco's death. For 42 years it was on loan to MOMA in New York City. A parallel is the great poet León Felipe (1884-1968), who died in exile in Mexico City. In a heartrending poem, he declares that

Franco has the *property*, but is mute because the poet has taken away the song.

Censorship was a major issue during the *dictadura*. Book banning was prevalent. For years theater people in Spain who wanted to learn about Bertolt Brecht needed to be devious. They could learn German to read his theater and theory in the author's language, or perhaps travel to France to see plays performed, or become friends with the Diosdado acting family that had lived in Argentina, where Spanish translations of Brecht readily appeared. Those books were smuggled into Spain and were on loan *sotto voce*. These secret maneuvers explain how Brecht's plays reached the Spanish stage almost overnight when the ban was lifted in 1965.

Censorship of plays in performance was more severe and arbitrary than censorship of books. Subsequent to a 1941 law, foreign films had to be dubbed, not presented in their original languages with subtitles. That led to invasive rewriting of scripts. Costumes of actresses were altered to be more modest and, in some cases, the number of women in the productions was reduced. An article in *Newsweek* in January, 1951 highlighted that, in Spain, "What's funny isn't."

In the first decade after Franco's victory, the Spanish stage allowed some younger writers of clever comedies but did not welcome original serious drama by Spaniards. That barrier was surmounted in 1949 by the realistic *Story of a Stairway* (*Historia de una escalera*), a text submitted anonymously that won the Lope de Vega prize. How surprised the censors must have been to learn that the author, Antonio Buero Vallejo (1916-2000), had spent years in prison after the war, initially under a death sentence. In the next few decades Buero Vallejo had achieved great fame internationally and in Spain, but long had to use allegorical works, sometimes with historical themes, in order to veil his criticism of Francoism.

A police state—one that promotes "law and order"—creates an atmosphere not of safety but of fear. In 1961, with other young American women who were studying in France, I went to Spain for the first time. We arrived at night in a train station and took a cab. We were stopped by uniformed men armed with bayonets who demanded to know where we were going. Fortunately we had a hotel reservation. How would they have responded if we'd had no answer for them?

Little by little during the dictatorship, conditions eased somewhat, but repression continued. Women did not have reproductive freedom. Contraceptives were outlawed. Voluntary sterilization, even to protect a woman's life, was illegal. Homosexuality was a crime. The model divorce law that was put in place during the Second Republic (1931-36) was rescinded, retroactively. Divorced couples were once again married; children born to second marriages were suddenly illegitimate.

Elena Quiroga (1921-1995) probes the psychological difficulties created by erasing divorce records. The word divorce is barely mentioned in her 1954 novel *Algo pasa en la calle* and is not mentioned at all in the reviews published at that time in Spain. Given the complex, Faulknerian structure of Quiroga's novel, perhaps the critics did not read the work thoroughly or perhaps they were trying to avoid problems themselves with censorship. While doing research on Quiroga, I asked a Spanish colleague at Rutgers what he knew about divorce in Spain. He quickly said that it had never existed. There are reasons why Spain with its 2007 Law of Historical Memory is still trying to recover its past.

I asked Quiroga how she had managed to get her radical novel past the censor. She replied that the man who interviewed her said that such a young, attractive woman would not write anything inappropriate. She did not disagree and therefore her novel was not scrutinized like many other works that were examined and rejected.

Arrabal himself has lived most of his life in France. He went there initially seeking treatment for lung disease, ultimately remained and married Luce Moreau, a French woman who for years taught Spanish at the Sorbonne; Fernando and Luce have two children, who are decidedly French. They were not force-fed religion as their father had been, in Spain, where his upbringing was permeated by National Catholicism. Franco enforced Catholicism on one and all. Protestant missionaries were banned from Spain for years while he was supreme leader.

Arrabal's plays were not welcomed in Spain because they were avant-garde, too experimental to please Spanish critics and spectators. He achieved early successes in France and other countries, but not in Spain under Franco. At first he was clearly *persona non grata*; he was jailed in 1967 during a trip home and released only because of international outrage. Later his works were staged by INTAR in New York, a theater run by Cuban-Americans, in part because he had organized protests when the Castro regime imprisoned a celebrated writer in Cuba.

For the INTAR opening performance of *The Body-Builder's Book of Love* (*Breviaro de amor de un halterófilo*, trans. Lorenzo Mans), Rutgers students and faculty had the pleasure of traveling from New Jersey to New York City with Fernando and Luce Arrabal in our chartered bus. That happy occasion was the subject of many conversations on our campus in 1990.

Ironically, Arrabal, who was banned by the dictator, was honored by King Juan Carlos I of Spain when Franco was gone. One year in France, on my way to Spain, Arrabal told me that he was giving a presentation on poetry at a large municipal theater in Madrid and urged me to get my ticket quickly. I did, and even so was seated in the middle of the auditorium. People were waiting in long lines to hear him speak, even with standing room only. Franco was gone and Spain was no longer mute.

Although much of what Arrabal dreamed of when he wrote his letter to Francisco Franco has since come to pass, it is still essential to foreground the terrible episodes of past dictatorships. Younger Spaniards may not understand the messages hidden in the allegorical works that were written during the Francoist period. In 1970, Buero Vallejo in *The Sleep of Reason* (*El sueño de la razón,* trans. Marion Peter Holt) used the opposition in 1823 between painter Francisco Goya and the absolutist power of King Ferdinand VII to convey a strong message about conflict between Franco and creative artists in contemporary Spain. In 1986, when the English translation was staged in Philadelphia at the Wilma Theater, my graduate students attended. In the following class, I asked the Spaniards among them what that play would have meant to audiences in Spain when it was first performed. They had no idea. Finally an older student from Argentina said it made her think of Juan Perón.

How quickly the memory of Franco disappeared and how frightening that is to those of us who hear the rhetoric today of politicians who praise dictators and wish to emulate them.

Phyllis Zatlin
Emerita
Rutgers University

Letter to General Franco

from

Fernando Arrabal

Complete text of the letter sent to Francisco Franco, 18
March, 1971, published in France, 1972.
Translated and annotated by Peter Thompson.

Paris, 18 March, 1971

Don Francisco Franco
El Pardo Palace,
Spain

Most Excellent Sir:
I write this letter with love.
Without the slightest hate or rancor, I must tell you that you are the man who has done the most to hurt me.
I am very afraid, as I begin to write you:
I fear this modest letter (which stirs me from head to toe) is too fragile to actually reach you;
that it might not arrive in your hands.
I believe your own suffering is infinite;
only a being who suffers this much could inflict so much pain in turn;
pain abides not only in your political and military life, but also in your amusements:
you paint shipwrecks and your favorite game is the killing of rabbits, doves and tuna fish.
Your biography, so strewn with corpses! — In Africa, in Asturias, during the civil war, and the

post-war...[1]

Your whole life shrouded in the mildew of mourning. I picture you surrounded by doves without feet, black garlands, dreams gnashing with blood and death.

I want you to transform, to change,

save yourself, yes,

that is to say, that you might be happy in the end—

you might abandon the world of repression, hate, prison, those both good and evil who surround you today.

Maybe I have some remote hope that you will hear me: indeed, when I was a child they took me to a ceremony you presided over.

At your entrance, amid applause, the authorities were glaringly obsequious.

Then a little girl, much preparation behind her, approached you and held out a bunch of flowers. Next she began reciting a poem (thoroughly rehearsed)... But, suddenly, overcome with emotion, she began to cry. You said, caressing her cheek:

---

[1] As many as 50,000 killed by the fascists, *after* the war.

"Don't cry, I'm a man like any other."

Is it possible your words held anything more than pure cynicism?

* * *

I am not part of that legion of Spaniards who, at the end of the civil war, crossed the snow-draped Pyrenees.

Like my friend Enrique who was eleven months old at the time.

Stomach dry, fear burbling in them, they were seeking the summits, fleeing the depths of fury.

How much anonymous heroism!

How many mothers, on foot, their children in their arms!

Later, through the long years, through these last epochs, how many have fled?

How many emigrated?

* * *

Centuries ago, there lived in Ávila an eight year old girl.

One day she took her little brother by the hand and escaped from the house.

They ran, over fields and mountains.

Finally their father caught up with them. He asked her, "Why did you run away?"

"I wanted to leave Spain."

"But... why?"

"To achieve glory!"

What this girl—Saint Theresa[2]—said could have been said by so many who fled—hundreds of thousands

along with the Goyas, Picassos, Buñuels...

the same could have been said by all of us who, in 1955, left your blackened Spain.

To conquer glory, in the most fascinating sense of that word.

This girl who escaped in search of apotheosis was later to suffer, in her flesh and in her soul, under the blows of the intolerance of that era: the Inquisition.

* * *

In hopes that you'll see not the slightest pride in me.

---

[2] Franco had a special relation with St. Theresa of Ávila, the 16th century Carmelite mystic. During the civil war, in 1937, her left hand, a sacred relic said to be incorruptible, was stolen by Franco. He is said to have kept it by his bedside for the rest of his life (hence the reference on page 100).

In no way do I feel superior to anyone, and still less than that, superior to you; we are all the same.

You must listen to this voice that comes to you flying across half of Europe,[3] and bathed in emotion.

What I'm going to write you in this letter could be said by the majority of the people of Spain, if their lips weren't sealed

it is what the poets say privately

But they can't proclaim out loud what the heart screams to them

They risk prison

That is why so many left.

* * *

Your regime is one link more in a chain of intolerances that began centuries ago in Spain.

I would like you to become more conscious of this situation

and, thanks to this, for you to take off the gags and handcuffs that imprison the majority of the Spanish people.

That is the aim of my letter:

---

3 Arrabal is writing from France (1971).

That you change.

You deserve to save yourself, like all men: from Stalin to Gandhi

You deserve to be happy — how can you be, knowing the terror your regime has imposed and continues to impose?

You must suffer greatly, to create this intolerance and reprisal all around you.

You deserve salvation, being happy.

Spain has to finally stop poisoning its people.

How much ash, how many tears, how much slow death among slag-heap funerals and the sound of rotting church bells?

* * *

A few centuries ago there was a country where Arab philosophers elaborated the deepest thinking of their tradition;

while, a few streets away, Jews raised that monument, the Kabbala

and Christians that marvel, the polyglot Bible.

That country was Spain.

Her kings were named, for example, Alfonso X, The Wise, or Ferdinand III, The Saint.

This last monarch dubbed himself "King of The Three religions"

(and I'm proud to have his name).

Imagine the Spain of today accepting the three most popular currents of thought in the country and sponsoring them with complete freedom: democracy, Marxism and religious devotion.

If you delegated your power to the people, what jubilation!

What happiness for you!

What happiness for all Spaniards.

But that constructive tolerance that impregnated the Middle Ages was to end brutally

The *Reyes Católicos*[4] arrived on the scene

they expelled two of the three religions

proclaimed Christianity the obligatory religion

and by fire and blood tried to exterminate Judaism and Islam.

The blackest night in history was falling in Spain,

The burning-stakes of the Inquisition were set afire and its sinister intolerances are still glowing.

And unto this day there reigns a silence of

---

4 Ferdinand and Isabella

charred flowers and infinite prison bars, like a muffled swarm of spiders in our brains.

Even in today's Spain some are rotting in dungeons for their crimes of opinion,

for proclaiming out loud an idealism kindled in the heart

for petitioning in the most pure and sincere way for a different system of rule in our country.

* * *

Whenever someone speaks of these true grievances that cause so much pain in my soul, the organs of your press declare that this is nothing but the Black Legend.[5]

Thanks to that label… all is taken care of.

For centuries now, in Spain, we have wanted to hide mountains of excrement behind a dainty lace fan.

Like Juana The Mad who, crazy with love, hid the decomposing body of Felipe the Fair, her idolized husband.

The *Reyes Católicos* put a yoke and arrows in their coat of arms.

---

5 This was long-standing propaganda, largely British and protestant, directed against Spain and Portugal.

Centuries later, the sole political party,
the party you leaned on for years,
would brandish the same coat of arms.

The yoke and arrows.

United one more time: this is the shield of the Falange.[6]

This gives me hope.

What if History were giving a sign, for us to better understand her?

And this coat of arms, this yoke and these arrows, might be only the parenthesis that has enclosed Spain in her long night of dogmatism?

Is it ending?

And a rebirth beginning?

* * *

I'm going to share a biography with you:

that of a man who has only known a Spain ruled by you.

Among a thousand examples

Like one of my four friends

with whom I created the "Academy"

an Academy of our own which, in the Madrid of

---

[6] The nationalist group—its Spanish arm founded by José Antonio Primo de Rivera—was an early ally of Franco.

the 1950s, at our age, twenty, allowed us a kind of exaltation in life.

With these friends, when we planned to place a laurel wreath (which we bought in a grocery store) on the neglected tomb of Velazquez, and with those who joined me to read Lorca's poems and those of Miguel Hernández, and with whom I argued till dawn to discover how the country might find equality and justice

Here we have the four:

José Luis came out of the civil war an orphan; his father and mother succumbed , victims of your army.

The father and grandfather of Eduardo were condemned to death and shot by your coreligionists.

Luis's father was taken prisoner, as an officer in the republican army at the fall of Madrid, and, despite the promises made to his superior, the republican General Casado, was condemned to death and assassinated.

José's parents, like his mother's parents, were able—after the harshest penalties, and three years of jail and concentration camps—to save themselves.

In my immediate family, you are the one—or your regime—responsible for the sentencing and mysterious disappearance of my father

and for the execution of his brother in Palma, Mallorca.

The families of my neighbors,

my companions,

all the families I know,

all

were wiped out in the same way.

Today, when the world is scandalized by ten or twenty executions for political reasons in some "under-developed" country

what comes into your head?

For weeks

and months

and years

and even without war as an excuse,

in the middle of peacetime,

the repressive apparatus continued, on your orders, condemning and slaughtering thousands of Spaniards,

reclaiming, as if the broken walls needed still

more blood, even those who had fled abroad and whom the Nazis handed over—

a dense mourning of raucous hyenas, slag and pus drooled down over the men of Spain

You said yourself, in those days:

"If we have to we will kill half the country."

Read my words.

None of this is spoken to you with rage.

I'm telling you what I believe to be true.

I am writing to you with love, I repeat.

What hatred could I have for you? :

You are nothing but a paper tiger, the power is the people

But you should be conscious, so I think, of where you come from,

of the harm you've caused,

of the pain your institutions cause.

Your reasons are well known:

"The Republic was skidding, in the middle of the greatest chaos, toward anarchy and Marxist atheism. Human rights were not guaranteed. 'Decent people' could not live in peace. Arbitrary arrests were increasing, attempted assassinations, revolutionary strikes. The bullet in the neck, as in the case of Calvo Sotelo,[7] perfectly illustrates what was going on. A climate of insecurity and anarchy was driving Spain mad, and was dragging her to her death."

That's what you have said to justify your coup d'état.

Spain was in a state of pure barbarity, you say…

…My opinion is that it was you who introduced an incomparable barbarity…

that of the *Reyes Católicos,*

that of the Inquisition.

I don't believe that there are the good on one side, and the bad on the other.

There simply exist blind violence and victims bathed in ashes.

Spain throngs with the righteous, armed to the teeth,

inquisitors,

implacable chiefs stiff with authority

and, above all, men who are always right and who want to impose their "right" on the rest—if necessary by fire and blood.

---

7 A former Finance Minister, Sotelo was shot in July, 1936 (the act was, itself, a reprisal by a leftist); the war began on July 18.

If I had been a German youth in the 1930s I would have written a letter like this to Hitler.

And today I'm writing to you, without hubris.

* * *

I'm going to relate, as I was telling you, a biography—the one I know best:

mine.

When the attack on the Spanish Republic began I was only four years old:

throughout my entire conscious life you have been in charge of Spain.

What a deserted country, how lonely her men are, what a long nightmare! 35 years buried among sirens.

The coup d'état (the uprising) began on July 18, 1936.

But in Melilla,[8] where my family and I were living, it launched early, on the 17th, a total surprise.

My family was about to live the tragedy of the civil war and the drama of the years that followed in a kind of summary of the entire population's woe.

---

8 A Spanish outpost (as it still is) on the north coast of Africa; Franco had been in charge of troops in Morocco.

When my father was arrested,
like all those in Melilla who (for others in Spain) had a reputation as liberals or republicans or Marxists,
there was nothing he could do to defend his ideas:
the surprise of the coup d'état rendered him indecisive.
It didn't matter.
The insurrectionists arrested him, and, immediately,
condemned him to death
with the extravagant accusation of "military rebellion."
He was one case among thousands and hundreds of thousands.
How many men—surprised in bed, at work, at the table, eating—were arrested?!
Many were assassinated without any kind of hearing.
I'm remembering the most illustrious: Federico García Lorca.
The majority were executed without any trial:
men,

women,

boys,

girls,

(Read the testimony of one of your soldiers, in *Fiesta*)

The lucky ones were given a parody of a trial

which ended, most times, with a death penalty for the accused.

As in the era of the Inquisition, death was the sanction for a crime of opinion.

Thus were many assassinated in the little town of Melilla.

In the whole of Spain so many followed them.

When there was some form of judgment the trial lasted a few minutes—

the accused defended by an enemy of his ideas, someone with no legal expertise,

someone who had received a copy of the charges only hours before the proceeding,

who, at the same time, had to defend anywhere up to thirty men whose lives hung in the balance,

a defender who, as an entire defense, in most cases, simply recognized the "extremely grave crimes" of the accused and begged clemency; but so many times the "defense" was even more hostile than the charges themselves.

In this way hundreds of men in Melilla were "judged"

hundreds of thousands in Spain.

Men who, so many times, were condemned to death

and assassinated (is there any other word for it?)
up against a cemetery wall.

One case among others:

A man was condemned to death by a Military Tribunal a few days after the war

Accused of having killed his village priest.

The remarkably short trial was just winding up when a robed figure burst into the room and declared that he was that very priest, and that in fact the reason he hadn't been killed in that "red zone" was the intervention of the condemned man.

The Tribunal huddled together again to deliberate, and shortly afterwards delivered the new verdict:

The accused had his death sentence commuted to life in prison, on the grounds that a man who was important enough in a red zone to save a priest was a significant enough red to deserve to spend the rest of his life in prison.

Indeed this poor man died in a prison in Burgos many years later:

How many men have disappeared forever,

of whom not a trace remains of the sacrifice—involuntary—of their lives.

How many yielded up their lives in the silence of bolts and bars, and then oblivion flattened them like a locomotive with no memory

Men swallowed forever by the earth.

Men who have left no trace in any arch of triumph,

in any history book,

Men who died, most of them, shouting *"Viva la libertad!"*...

and who will never again be spoken of by anybody.

Whose "martyrdom" was hidden for years by their families,

for fear of repression, until it was lost to memory.

These are the fathers of so many men of my generation.

Of us, who make up

the post-franquismo era.

Yes, you have to forget all this, as they say nowadays, and I do forget;

You have to look to the future and we can't anchor our lives in bitterness.

Your coreligionists have asserted that the violence created by the "uprising" and all its barbarism provoked, in turn, unjustifiable excesses by those in the red zone;

what we all know is that they didn't mete out punishments after winning.

The savagery of your operations has not paused even 32 years after your victory:

A few months ago in Burgos we saw men tortured and chained during their very trial, men the judges wouldn't allow to defend themselves

All this, as is often said and repeated, can and must be forgotten,

yes but with one condition:

that this combat never be seen as a crusade; nor its adherents seen as heroes or martyrs; nor the republicans as bandits.

Let it all be forgotten: Sure: after we condemn this war (the blemish we still bear).

And after you recognize, publicly and solemnly, that immense crimes were and are committed in your name.

The idealism of many of the combatants is recognized... the barbarism employed must itself be recognized and forever forbidden.

* * *

When I mention to my friends the need to write you a letter, they tell me I'm too optimistic and that...

"The leopard can't change its spots"[9]

All share the opinion that a man who has presided—like you—over so much horror can't about-face and recognize the crimes that have been and still are perpetrated in his name.

Any man can be touched by grace.

And why not you, who suffer so much,

You, in turn, who overflow with pain.

* * *

I was telling you about my father,
how he was condemned to death.

---

9 The rhyming Spanish, *genio y figura, hasta la sepultura*, is even more pointed as to human character.

Like so many others!

But he had the good fortune—after eight months in death's waiting room—to see his sentence commuted to thirty years and a day.

Do you know that in Peñon del Hacho, where he was incarcerated, they locked the prisoners in little iron cages?

Meanwhile, I was four years old... and, when the war ended, seven.

All I could do was be a child witness to a flaming brazier and death-frenzy that I couldn't analyze and that left its mark on my flesh and my soul, like a fiery branding iron.

So many children, like me, witness to the same spectacles!

Kids who dreamed of dynamite rattles and firing squads by their cradles

In my memory there linger precise and unforgettable incidents from the war... of its repression,

of terrors,

of panics,

of accusations,

sons denouncing their fathers,

brothers fighting against each other,
fanaticism,
censorship (letters always opened, cautious conversations, fearful footsteps),
fanaticism:
we heard about soldiers who adorned their waists with the ears of republican militants, the ears hanging like war trophies from their belts,
quavering echoes arrived, of the massacre in Badajoz, in the middle of the bull ring, where the blood flowed in torrents of slaughtered life,
of prisoners beating their heads against the walls to escape torture, in death's mercy,
of women and children who covered almost 300 miles terrified and on foot, to escape the vanguard of your army.
Daily life was colored by the same climate:
In the Churches, devout women dragged themselves to the altar on their knees, bloodying their legs,
in religious processions fragile old women dragged great steel balls on chains, ripping the skin off their ankles;
your newspapers told us, in lurid detail, of the

atrocities—real or not, but either way planting the same trauma in our child brains—of the "reds,"

the radio broadcast the voices of your Army's generals, proclaiming that not only were they going to liquidate all the republicans but that all their wives would be raped.

Even the holidays were impregnated with blood and death:

in the processions, to give the illusion of an everlasting miracle, they put doves at the feet of the effigies—doves that never flew away because "such was the spiritual power of the Virgin."

In reality they had pierced the eyes of the doves with needles and severed the nerves of their wings, and thus, trembling and blind, terrified, they stayed with their feet clutching the toes of the statue.

Those were the times when your news organs (never contradicted) proclaimed that the Virgin had covered your rebel army crossing the straits of Gibraltar with her miraculous cloak... when in reality it was Hitler's Junkers that protected your landing.

In this climate of hatred, fear and falsehood we

lived out the three years of the war.

And the perpetual victory raised ever higher the barbed-wire, wounding with echoless blades the solitude of Spain.

* * *

The day the struggle ended, a few hundred people assembled in the main square of Ciudad Rodrigo, the town where we lived;

we were listening, in silence, to the last stage of the war.

You read it out, if I recall rightly,

in a clear voice, with no particular feeling,

you proclaimed that the war was over

that the Red army had been disarmed.

There was, after this communiqué, a moment or two of sinking in;

but soon your entourage was loudly applauding,

as they knew how to do,

which is to say: giving the tacit order, to all those present, to do the same.

So then the whole plaza clapped;

and then sang the National Anthem, with their arms out straight.

It seemed to me that many were glancing toward the prison.

I even had the impression that they directed their gaze toward this prison with tenderness, with complicity; toward those men crammed into Ciudad Rodrigo's penitentiary, whose cries we often heard from its moat.

One day when we were playing among the gun placements next to the prison we asked one of the guards:

"Why are the prisoners screaming?"

And the guard, as if ashamed, tried to joke:

"Because they don't want to climb the stairs three by three."

In those days there was howling in all the prisons.

And those cries were the muffled tom-tom of the daily routine.

The conditions were Dantesque.

And even if they have somewhat improved, they are still, to the eye of any civilized being, intolerable.

I've talked with prisoners both common and political, and they've told me about the camps and the jails of those times.

While the world—preoccupied with the world war—forgot about Spain and her agony, men in the camps and prisons were treated in subhuman ways, and nobody saw or intervened.

It was an era when prisons received fifty times the normal number of inmates.

Each prisoner had about a foot of space for sleeping:

by the hundreds, in the corridors, the condemned slept, jammed together;

turning around was a problem: it meant waking up your two neighbors, who in turn woke up... etc. So, at various times during the night the whole row would change position, after one of the prisoners shouted "Ventas direction!"

* * *

Echoes drifted to our ears as children—and later, as youths—of medieval punishments,
vendettas,
men humiliated,
wounded,
tortured.

Despite total silence in the press, we knew
that, in one cemetery or another, they had killed
so many prisoners on a certain night, or that, in
another one they had buried a whole group.[10]

They spat on the ones they had shot

We knew the prisoners had to eat and urinate in
the same sardine tins;

that many died of hunger;

that others perished in the camps,[11] simply worn
out.

In Madrid, where I went to live when I was nine,
even the middle schools and parochial schools
were turned into prisons.

For example the Escolapios de San Antón y
Porlier.

Spain was nothing but a jail made up of little
jails, all hurtling toward Hell.

We knew that in the winters, severe ones,
especially in Teruel and Burgos, where, for

---

10 The Law of Historical Memory (*Ley de la Memoria Histórica*, 2007) has advanced the drive to recover bodies from long-known burial sites (both single and mass graves).

11 Arrabal has clarified with us which camps are meant—those where the franquistas rounded up republicans. Almost as notorious were those by which France responded to the mass of refugees.

months, the temperature drops below freezing,

the prisoners, with no heating system whatsoever

(like nowadays, in fact: they tell me Spain is the only country in Europe where the prisons don't have heat)

and no more shelter than a couple of blankets, were literally freezing to death.

* * *

I would so love all this to be untrue!

If you could prove to me that all the echoes that terrified my childhood and youth (confirmed, since, by the books I read while abroad) were pure invention...

* * *

They enrolled kids—who at that time (1944, 1945) were nine or ten years old—in the paramilitary units of the Falange.

There we learned to sing

"Long live the revolution

long live the Falange of the J.O.N.S.";[12]

---

12 The *Juntas de Ofensiva Nacional Sindicalista*, formally joined to the Falange; both proclaimed "socialist" leanings.

to call each other comrade
and to hate Art, England and Russia.
They jammed us into blue shirts,
to remind us of the workman's blue uniform,
while the young lords of the Falange, who spoke of themselves as pro-worker, went off to create a unionist revolution.

And they taught us to denounce, and asked us to denounce our neighbors.

Like Toledo's Inquisitor, who used to watch the chimneys of the city from the hilltops, on Friday nights, to see who was observing the sabbath—in the same way, Falange members suspected and surveilled.

How many times have I seen an old woman dragged to some squadron's barracks and shaved bald because she didn't know how to sing Cara al Sol.[13]

How many kids my age were locked in the Falange's dog houses after being given half a liter of castor oil—because they had smiled during one of the official ceremonies.

How many savagely beaten for not making their

---
13 "Face to The Sun."

stiff-arm salute with the required conviction.

Never mind those who, ratted on for their "more serious" intentions, went directly to prison.

So many things I wish I could forget.

* * *

There's something I'd like to tell you, in some detail:

I was living in Madrid. In 1946.

I was fourteen.

One fine day, at San Antón's, where I was in eighth grade, the Political Science professor (required subject)—that is, the person who was attempting to make fascists of us all—

told us we had to go to a demonstration.

to "support" Spain against the UN, which was moving toward a boycott of our country,

we were to go "with the whole of Madrid" to the Plaza de Oriente.

Class by class, and under the threat of severe punishment, we were lined up and aimed toward the Plaza.

Instead of going directly, those who were looking after us made us go by way of Plaza de Colón, the

Cibeles fountain, Calle Alcalá, etc.

Eventually I understood why we had to go in this wildly roundabout way from Calle de Hortaleza (Saint Anthony's School) to the Plaza de Oriente:

So that all of Madrid would seem flooded with "spontaneous" parades.

They made us shout slogans that, for the most part, meant absolutely nothing to us.

Miraculously, my memory has stored a few of these:

"They might have ONE, but we have two."

"UNO; ONU; DOS: los testículos."

"Thorez is a bull."[14]

Only years later would I figure out who Thorez was, who provoked such rage in our educators.

When we got to the Plaza de Oriente we numbered, it seemed (and it's not improbable), half a million.

In factories and offices workers were enlisted in the same way.

And thus—with identical threats—the old playwright Jacinto Benavente was brought to the

---

14 A play on O.N.U., Spanish for the U.N.; Thorez was the leader of the Communist Party in France.

Plaza; this ancient author and the author who was then being born (me) met in the crush of the Plaza perhaps to transmit to each other in their very domain, in our domain (theater itself, that is): our repulsion at the intolerance that surrounded us.

Among the claws, daggers, and leather boots, which left room neither for rivers nor stars, the old man in chains and the boy looked at each other like sheep in winter.

* * *

Months later another political event was to occur, one I remember with great emotion

They had organized a referendum; it was supposed to happen in 1946.

I don't recall the basis of it.

Any publicity in favor of either abstention or a NO vote entailed a jail sentence.

For weeks the whole country was invaded with the official propaganda: "Vote Yes"

Naturally, no one dared to suggest (even in private) abstaining or voting NO

Next to my house on Calle de La Madera there was a polling place:

right on Calle La Luna, almost across from where the next street begins.

The morning of the referendum, in the polling place and out in the street, an impressive line had formed.

All those men and women from the densely populated streets—Pez, San Roque, etc.—were lining up with their clearly visible Yes ballots.

How can I ever forget those fearful faces, my neighbors, afraid they might not be able to cast those ballots!

What panic in their faces. Such emotion, seeing them so fragile, so humiliated.

All hoped to be spared the reprisals meted out—according to officious word of mouth—to any who didn't vote.

Poor people, poor people as great as this earth—and so threatened!

Such were politics in Spain, in your name.

* * *

Everything took on this grotesque and tragic aspect.

The speeches, addressing the Masonico-liberal,

judeo-democratico-marxist plot,
   the xenophobic attacks on perfidious Albion,
   against atheist Russia
   etc.
   In that climate of vengeance, fears, and lies we youths were just coming into life.
   Any criticism was forbidden.
   Doubting the existence of God risked being yanked from school.
   Condemning Catholicism incurred the worst dangers,
   The slightest criticism of either you or your government: jail.
   Books simply taught errors
   or silenced any thinking that didn't square with your form of government.
   Censorship ruled in every area.
   Your government was afraid of everything.
   In my Literature textbook, the most important writers were only allowed a few defamatory lines.
   About Voltaire, for example, the book had this to say, categorically:
   "A Satanic monster who dreamt of destroying the Church. All his works are in the Index Librorum

Prohibitorum."

The greatest French poets (Baudelaire and Rimbaud) could be found on a list of noted scoundrels.

Any philosophical, political, literary or scientific theory that didn't align with the official dogma was condemned in the briefest terms.

Education had a double mission:

—not informing us,

—condemning.

Thus an entire generation of students, mine, was trained.

Imagine what was going on in less privileged schools.

In those days, when misery was so widespread that it wasn't rare to see someone faint in the street, from hunger...

What tragic times... and at times tragicomic.

In one of those years the premiere of the film *Gilda* was interrupted, in the Music Palace in Madrid, by shouts of "Long Live Christ The King!," because the film—cut by the censors—was considered atheistic.

* * *

Back then there was a formula, sinister but at the same time said with tenderness, that you spilled before any kind of confrontation with a policeman or franquista official:

"No, sir, I've been right-wing my whole life."

That is, it wasn't enough to simply be on the right, but you almost had to demonstrate that you had been there from birth.

This was more serious than it might seem.

23 years after the end of the war, Julián Grimau[15] was condemned to die

and executed

for misdeeds (imaginary) committed (according to his assassins) decades earlier.

That is, they reproached Julián Grimau with not having been "on the right" his whole life: this was made clear in his extremely short hearing; this was the only thing made clear.

All Spain was "on the right for their entire lives,"

or could fake it,

or was in jail,

---

15   The trial was an international *cause célèbre*; Grimau's activities as a communist, before, during and after the Civil War, made his case complicated and problematic.

or in exile.

I can draw another parallel with the era of the Inquisition and Torquemada in which, following a governmental edict, all Spaniards had to be Christians,

"Christians for their entire lives..."; at that time the term was "old Christians"...! and how ironic of history: later the title "old shirt"[16] would appear, to designate those on the right

Jews and Muslims had to camouflage themselves as Christians,

or be faced with the fiery stakes of the Inquisition,

or be exiled forever.

This system you impose brings with it more grief (and crime, alas!):

it creates hypocrisy and lying,

it creates hypocrites and liars at the point of the bayonet.

How is it possible that the kind of conversion your regime exacts from the poor population fulfills you?

---

16 *Camisa vieja*, in its strictest sense, meant someone who had belonged to the Spanish Falange before the Civil War.

Who could possibly believe that, through some kind of magic spell, all of Spain—whose majority favored republican democracy or liberal monarchy or Marxism—would suddenly embrace a military dictatorship with such warmth and unanimity?

Do your collaborators believe this?

Or maybe they think that, after several eons of political totalitarianism, all freedom of thought can be uprooted from the country?

We were children manipulated, and men in search of speech

What silence under every roof!

* * *

Many have told me it's useless to write you;

others opine that, in turning to you, I give the impression that you might not know what all Spaniards know

—no matter.

All I want is for you to read this sincere letter—which I hope might be constructive—and that you manage to hear it, even if only because of my words' sincerity.

Others assert that the police in your service will

try to exact vengeance or make my life even more impossible than they make it already.

That there will be reprisals.

What does it matter!?

What, or who, could prevent my sending you this testimony, when I believe it's essential that it reach you ?

* * *

In our younger years the absence of criticism, the ambient dogmatism, was creating an unreal, nightmarish situation.

Nobody, ever, (then or since) publicly made even the most harmless statement against this situation.

Contrary to what one might think, this brainwashing produced reactions completely opposite to those intended.

Secretly, we were all
convinced
that any official proclamation, or any government information, was always completely false.

That is how we could deny even obvious truths—because they came to us stained by the official seal.

We distrusted everything;

we are a generation of skeptics.

And, in a mirrored way,

we were ready to publicly "recognize" the worst aberrations, since this approval was necessary so we could earn our daily bread.

Two certificates were needed for everything you wanted:

—one, certifying loyalty to the regime, issued by Falangist officials;

—the other, of "good conduct"; (that is, of being Catholic and devout in observance), which the parish priest gave.

So many times we swore loyalty and Catholic faith without believing a single word of it, because this oath was a barrier that had to be crossed simply to have a job, or to pursue studies.

In 1949, when I wanted to be employed in a private firm (La Papelera Española), both certificates were required—as they were for all Spaniards who were simply trying to eat from the sweat of their labors.

All tenaciously stamped, so we might enter—

wilted and submissive—into the steel labyrinth.

* * *

The sterile climate of this universal "amen," with no trace of criticism, brought with it extremes as unimagined as they were comical.

In the midst of a campaign of exacerbated nationalism, in which all the organs of opinion proclaimed

that Spain was the best country in the world

that everything Spanish was the most marvelous

there occurred something you may have forgotten but which, it seems to me, exemplifies the situation of cretinization this lack of criticism had brought about.

Suddenly, the highly-placed decided that "Spanish cognac" was the best in the world

and it was a national shame that it wore a French name

that it was called cognac.

They hit upon a national contest, to come up with a name for the incomparable Spanish cognac.

For weeks the authorities pushed this issue, to try to galvanize the country.

Amidst "the greatest excitement" a jury was assembled, made up of the grandest names in Francoist culture, who were going to crown the winner

How great was the consternation of the patient populace when they learned that the winning name was "Jeriñac." A grotesque moniker sounding even more French than the previous one.

"Waiter, a jeriñac."

For months there was peril in not using the absurd name to order cognac in a café.

"Waiter! A jeriñac!"

* * *

This was the era in which you published "the greatest novel to come out of the Christian West": *Raza*[17]

which gave birth to a film of the same name "which was going to be a landmark in the history of film."

And an era in which, as a parallel, Picasso, Buñuel, Alberti etc. were deemed criminal

---

[17] Race.

impostors.

* * *

I spent several years after the war in schools under the Escuelas Pías:

Every class began with a prayer, as in all the public and private schools,

every classroom had your portrait, that of José Antonio, and between them, a Christ.

Every morning, lined up with all the other students in the school, we sang patriotic hymns, arms out straight—and ended with Vivas for you, and choruses of Up With Spain.

Government bureaucrats, and officials from the only party (the Falange) taught classes in political science, religion, and gym,

these subjects figuring into our curriculum with the same weight as mathematics or grammar;

thanks to them any critical thinking was to be suppressed,

and dogmatism instilled.

And these three subjects pursued us through all our years of studying

Not only in middle and high school, but also at

the universities.

In 1955, when I was winding up my law studies, I had to present myself for these brainwashing-examinations.

Which created a moment of hypocrisy.

And creates still: since nothing has changed

All students

who today are engineers, lawyers, doctors,

and the great majority of whom opposed your regime,

found themselves obliged to bury their ideas, their most noble and sincere beliefs, and to proclaim during these exams their "love of Francoism and Catholicism" to be allowed to finish their studies.

What official could be satisfied by this "conversion" that lasted only the time of an examination?

We were so used to this kind of abuse that all we did to show our hatred or contempt for it was to mutter jokes about the three "Marys" who, like three prostitutes, accompanied us throughout our student lives.

* * *

Was I an orphan, back then?

What happened to my father?

I think I have the right to explanations, from you and your ministers.

A man burying my feet in the sand. It was the beach, in Melilla. I remember his hands on my legs. I was three. The sun was shining—heart, diamond, and a bursting in infinite drops of water.

When I'm asked what person has most influenced me, I reply that it was a being of whom I can only manage to remember this: his hands on my feet: my father.

For years I have crisscrossed Spain seeking his letters, his pictures, his drawings. Each of these works awakes in me universes of silence and wailings cut through with tears.

After his death sentence in Melilla and its commutation to thirty years and a day, he was off to the prisons in Ceuta, Ciudad-Rodrigo and Burgos.

In Ceuta he tried to kill himself by slicing his veins; even now I can feel the warm trickle of his blood over my bare back.

On November 4, 1941, stricken with a "mental

disturbance," so they say, he was moved from the Central Prison to the mental health section of the Provincial Hospital of Burgos.

Fifty-four days later he escaped… and disappeared… perhaps forever.

In my wanderings I've met his jailers, nurses, his doctor… but neither his voice nor the look in his face live in my imagination.

The day he disappeared there were three feet of snow on the ground in Burgos, and the archives reveal that he carried no form of identification; he was wearing only pajamas.

My father had been born in Córdoba in 1903. His life, all the way up to his disappearance, is one of the most pitiful I know.

Calumny, silence and fire have not choked off this blood-voice that comes to me over the mountains and bathes me with light.

From all appearances, there are those who would make me pay for not renouncing my father. Woe unto those in whose heart lives nothing but violence.

For my part, I extend a fraternal hand to all those—whatever their thinking—who oppose

injustice. The same would have been said by
that man who left only the memory of his hands
burying my feet in the sandy beach at Melilla.

My father. Did he disappear forever?;
did the earth simply swallow him?
You are guilty of this; you must answer me.
And so many disappeared along with him!

* * *

And how many went mad as well.
Including those in universities, who came from well-off families.

How many students started acting strangely;
while others raved,
like the one who imagined there was a radio set in his chest transmitting military marches;
or that other one, a brilliant medical student, who suddenly abandoned all his studies to read only "children's books." And when someone advised him to keep studying, he replied in a robotic voice:

"Studying…? What for? What I need are children's books"
or that law student who, like a crazed Quijote,

launched a crusade in the Atheneum to demonstrate to us that our brains were circled with barbed wire and that it was extremely dangerous to move our heads in certain ways.

I remember a commercial seamstress whose salary barely allowed her to eat; she took refuge in a book of gastronomy which she read and reread to calm her hunger, the way some might use a pornographic novel to tamp down their sexual appetites.

Everything was crazy all around us... though it took on official forms!

All shows ended, by government order, with the national anthem and the traditional shouts of Viva Franco and Arriba España!

One day in the Carlos III theater in Madrid, at the end of the movie, we the audience—in a hurry and with absolutely no subversive intent—tried to skip this exercise and leave.

The police, immediately notified,

locked us in!

and, with arms out straight, we were forced to sing Cara al Sol—over and over and over.

* * *

It was a time of terror in every sphere:
to the point of hysteria:
political terror, naturally,
but also religious and sexual.

For example, the Employees' Center, a Catholic organization in Madrid, dedicated itself to surprising lovers who had secluded themselves in the shady environs of the Cuartel de la Montaña— to give them a sound beating, or douse them with buckets of cold water.

"... And the little pigs should be happy we don't tell the police."

Those years, those epochs of our unfolding childhood and our youth... how many managed to emerge from them undamaged?

A childhood bathed in stagnant water, and a heart wounded

I remember
that everyone
went to Mass
because there was no way out of it, as we said back then.

That alone is blasphemy!

But the real blasphemers are those who force the

majority to accept something that doesn't convince them.

For a curse involving God's name (He who was in the custody of the highly-placed) you went to prison or, with better luck, received a beating.

Everything I'm telling you is something I've seen, or heard

For example:

A bunch of young men, drunk, who were about to start military service, had the extremely bad idea of defecating in the pediment hole where the church's great cross was mounted…

they were condemned to twelve years in jail.

The God of Love was transformed, in the hands of your sycophants (forgive the expression), into the God of Vengeance and Hate.

Republicans and democrats at heart (in their own way, for idealism, for love of Spain) saw themselves obliged to enlist in the Falange, to go to Mass or to put up emblems and flags, if they didn't want to lose the modest jobs that provided food for their children.

Men forever humiliated!

You had to lie

to live with fakery

you had to pray and take communion just to get a job as doorman at one of the Ministries

you had to yell Viva! For the Revolución Nacional Sindicalista just to be allowed to sell cigarettes from a stall in a Madrid plaza[18]

So many poor, degraded, down-trodden men obliged to call black what they knew full well was white.

And these same men condemned to shame forever, before their own conscience.

So many men showing up again and again at demonstrations, meetings, churches, musters, because they feared it might be known one day that they had belonged to a labor union or a democratic party.

Anguished men asking their "well-connected" friends:

"There's no dossier on me, right?"

What fear, panic—having a police file on you

---

18 The full, awkward line is "a mutilated person's cart," a fairly common manifestation into the 21st century. The most famous vendor was Rosario Sánchez Mora, called "La Dinamitera"—celebrated for her expertise with explosives, and who lost her hand readying these against the fascists.

We all had a file.
The martyrs,
the heroes
were in exile and prisons.
Just as in the time of the Inquisition.
But I'd like to tell you about those other martyrs,
those martyred by silence:
modest men, shamed by an internal verdict,
who saw themselves as guilty for having betrayed their ideas,
and who just weren't lucid enough to realize they weren't hypocrites.
Because they had chosen neither betrayal or hypocrisy. They were *forced* to betray their ideas,
to display themselves as other than what they were thinking, or risk losing either
life
or their daily bread.
Among shadows, spurs, and threats, holding back their fury and their breath, an entire population's ideals and red daisies, withering.

* * *

A little while ago, three or four years,

a democratic playwright was living in Madrid.

As his theater hadn't gained any significant audience, in Spain or abroad, he found himself forced to work in television, to feed his family; his wife was pregnant at the time.

It became known in Madrid that, in Asturias—and with even more system and method than usual—torture reigned in the police stations and the mines;[19]

Atrocious echoes rolled in;

not even women escaped the ferocity of some of the police.

A group of intellectuals wrote a letter

destined for you and very respectful

taking every precaution not to transgress any norm either of Francoist law or of the Fuero de los Españoles,[20]

pointing out the facts

and suggesting steps to be taken

The Madrid playwright signed the text (note: it was a private letter, never to be published in Spain)

---

19 Asturias is a mining region. Note that this severe torture was being carried out in the late 1960s, thirty years after the war.
20 One of the keystones of the Francoist law code.

Immediately, a bureaucrat from Spanish Television informed him that if he didn't withdraw his signature he would lose his post or go to jail. Heroic, he replied that, if it had to be, he would die of hunger.

When he gave his wife the news of his expulsion from TV she was traumatized—and hemorrhaged.

Doctors verified that a second hemorrhage would cause a miscarriage.

Humiliated, the Madrid playwright returned to the boss's office.

The next day, the official press declared that it had been the reds who attached his signature to the letter, without his consent—since in fact he was a loyal Francoist.

He was restored to his job,
had his child
and, for added humiliation,
was forced to join the committee of theater censors.

And who among us would dare throw the first stone at him?

* * *

What happens to those who don't submit?

They join the anonymous troupe, the anonymous who oppose this regime.

Who remembers an official who resigned his post, refusing to sanction a crime with his signature?:

Nobody: now the man vegetates, doing the accounting for a small business.

Or that journalist, editor-in-chief of a newspaper, who quit rather than print news pieces that had been cut?:

Nobody: these days, to live, he runs a copying machine.

Or that consul who, during proceedings, suddenly "chose freedom"?:

Nobody: today he's living abroad, with neither hassles nor glory, waiting for a hypothetical change in Spain.

Neither History, capital H, nor the smaller history remembers them.

The artist who has chosen exile

and won't conform to your system

will see his works and his life swallowed as if by the very earth

Official Spain will persecute life and works relentlessly within the country

While abroad the "cultural attachés" invent all manner of calumnies to crush him.

* * *

Our best professors were in exile,

or prevented from teaching,

new ideas forbidden

the education of our generation couldn't have been worse

Children guided by steers, punished with sightless swords while locked in putrefying churches. Light imprisoned and hope destroyed.

The teaching methods were startling.

In all the Colegios de Los Escolapios I attended (San Antón, Getafe, Tolosa) students were subjected to corporal punishment.

Beatings were the pedagogical weapon.

Epic beatings

it wasn't unusual to see a teacher (or priest) strike a student with kicks and punches until he bled.

An education in the image and likeness of the times

And we ourselves, we children, reenacted in our games the violence we were witnessing
savage games, in which the martyrdom and torture of fellow students assumed great importance
and likewise the mutilation or execution of animals.

* * *

Echoes reached us from the prisons
in which—to prevent the condemned from yelling such subversive slogans as "Viva la Libertad!"—
muzzles
were strapped on
preventing them from saying anything before the bullets of the firing squad.
And these muzzles, still wet with panting and drool, were used again 24 hours later,
at the same walls in the same cemetery,
by a new group of victims.
Prisoners who were forced to confess before dying.
This brief and secret ceremony, between a

condemned man and a priest most often rendered fanatic by so much blood and hate, would end dramatically:

in the Burgos prison one of the condemned was slaughtered by blows on the head with a crucifix,

without anyone ever finding out what he could have told his confessor that so enraged him.

That's how they tried to bring us up:

with hammer blows from a crucifix.

That's how they wanted to stuff our heads:

with religion,

fatherland,

Francoism:

by blows with a crucifix.

For many, like the prisoner I'm describing, their heads exploded in lightning bolts of blood that then fell, drop by drop, from their shackles.[21]

This was (and, unfortunately, still is!) a Spain directed and dominated by the most rotten element of the Army

Since the battle of Rocroy, 1643,

The Spanish Army has lost every skirmish:

---

[21] "Shackles" is a metaphorical and less common use of *cascabeles*, "little bells."

in Spain, in Europe, in America, in the Pacific, in Africa

Any "glorious" deeds were accomplished by guerilla groups, as in the fight against Napoleon.

A band of poorly armed Moroccans kept the Spanish Army in check for years and years.

How many of this Army's battles does history inscribe under the heading "disaster."

Ineffective against foreign rivals, the gangrenous part of the Army has found only one enemy it could handle: the Spanish people

What a great revenge the internal wars were for these military felons, when, at last, their medals didn't decorate defeats

And what tremendous sadness, what great pain: the vanquished were the people, armed like rabbit hunters.

And I'm saying "the rotten or gangrenous part of the Army."

Because there's a certain lie your people have inserted in the dogma: "the entire Spanish Army rose up against the Republic." On the contrary, the truth is that the majority of officers (not to mention the troops) backed the Republic against your insurrection.

Your allies were: the Foreign Legion, the Moroccan mercenaries, the Italian fascists, the German Nazis... and a small element of the Spanish Army.

That's why the repression was so severe against soldiers:

—D. Domingo Batet Mestre, general in charge of the VIth region army, was assassinated by

Mola, who seized his command.

—D. Nicolas Molero Lobo, in charge of the VIIth region, was assassinated by his "successor."

—The captain general of the IInd region, D. José Fernández Villa, was shot by Queipo de Llano.

—In Granada, not only was García Lorca shot, but the military governor as well, D. Miguel Campins.

Likewise assassinated:

—captain general D. Enrique Salcedo

—general Núñez Prado, in Zaragoza

—inspector of the legion D. Luis Molina Galano, in Ceuta

—general Romerales, in Melilla

—general Caridad Pita, in La Coruña

—general Mena Zueco, in Burgos

—the high commissioner in Morocco, D. Arturo Alvarez Buylla, in Tetouan

—general Gómez-Caminero, in Salamanca

—general Lopez Viota, in Seville

—the director of the weapons factory in Asturias, D. José Franco Mussio

—Etc.

Only one of the commanding generals of the eight military regions joined the uprising

Of the 21 general officers (the highest rank in the Spanish Army) 17 remained loyal to the Republic.

Out of the 59 brigadier generals 42 chose the Republic.

Just as all the generals in the Guardia Civil, and the head of the Air Force, embraced the cause of republican law.

How many soldiers gave their blood for the Republic!

Never in History was there such a military bloodbath in defense of the Republic!

* * *

These days, according to your friends, the

situation isn't as dramatic as it was at war's end

Nonetheless:

Intolerance persists

Absence of any criticism is the law

For the thirty-five years you've been in power there has never been the slightest criticism aimed at your person or your form of government.

Read and reread this sentence, which seems impossible

Neither direct nor indirect, the slightest criticism

When a newspaper said that De Gaulle should resign, a couple of years ago, the paper was suspended because your censors felt that such an article could be considered an appeal for *you*

to hand over the reins.

Every commentary on radio, television or in the papers is always a favorable one, to your "crusade" and to the regime it installed.

They are all adulation, praises, bravos.

Tresses of bitter honey smothering Spain in a slimy silence

If no one criticizes, how can we progress?

How can we correct inevitable defects?

Is there such a thing as an infallible man?

The best Spaniards (only speaking, for now, of those who chose neither jail nor exile) carry on outside the formal organization of the country.

Poor Spain! A bodega reeking of urine where you eat surrounded by the barbed wire of mourning while a rabid dog sinks its fangs in your heart.

* * *

Censorship has its veto over the press, over art.
The people have no way to express themselves
to show what ails them
or to propose reforms.
For example:
the unions don't serve to defend workers, rather to harness them or oblige them to accept orders from the government.

In my business: the theater
the organizers in this union have never done anything to close the scandalous chapter in which antifrancoist writers cannot exercise their profession in Spain (and yet this right is protected by every law and charter)

rather, on the contrary, this union (whose purpose is to defend writers) is the one leading the campaign against their plays being produced in Spain.

They're not the defenders of writers, but your wolf-dogs ever ready to bite us if we don't stay mute and obedient in the middle of the flock.

* * *

Those who ought to be the representatives of the nation, in the legislative chambers, are hand-picked by you or else by such particular mechanisms
  that
  never (I'm saying *never*)
  has someone opposed to the government been able to enter the Cortes
  The mayors, governors, newspaper editors, union heads...
  any person who holds the slightest parcel of authority in Spain has had to guarantee loyalty to the official doctrine—and is stripped, ipso facto, of authority the second this fails.

The absence of criticism can lead to the greatest catastrophes, to losing all contact with reality, for the man who governs in this kind of adulation

An example:

Hitler's minister Albert Speer recounts in his Memoir that the Führer had ordered that everything be burned and destroyed in front of the advancing Allies. Speer, luckily, didn't carry out the order. When he went to visit Hitler a few weeks later, the following scene unfolded:

"Losing all control over myself (Speer relates, in his Memoir) I confessed to Hitler in a low voice that not only had I not destroyed everything, but that I had prevented any destruction.

For a few seconds the Führer's eyes filled with tears."

Like a sadistic child from whom they've confiscated a toy, the monster wept to know that Europe had not succumbed to flames.

Surrounded by ass-kissers he couldn't imagine being disobeyed even once.

What obscene courts of miracles[22] with his tragic viper-buffoons, presided over by a rusty and

---

22 Obscure, though some works of art have used it as title: a slum in 17th century France, where beggars who had faked lameness and blindness all day, returned at night and resumed walking and seeing normally.

dilapidated eagle!

* * *

In Spain the people have never been consulted.
No one knows what they think.
And when a referendum takes place it proceeds with so much fraud that
even the dead vote for the government.
So much fear of what the people think!
Fear of thinking, speaking or freely voting impregnates the life of this country.
In 1954, when I was working in a private office that had about a hundred employees, they held an election for union liaison—with absolutely no political ramifications, with results that could not shake the established order in the feeblest way—
and the meeting was carried out amid such pressures, as ridiculous as they were severe,
that the majority of employees (to stay out of trouble) advanced to the ballot box with a name brandished high, clearly visible: the name of the official candidate.
The threats were collective (withholding

overtime pay), and individual (dismissals, job changes, prison).

It gives the impression that the injustice that rules the country in its broad policies also informs the nation in its most microscopic acts.

It's logical that where the prisons torture, the children maltreat animals;

and no surprise that, mirroring the rigged referenda, there's cheating in every meaningless local election.

* * *

In that climate of oppression I was literally suffocating.

Since I couldn't breathe spiritually

I ended up having lung trouble and finally contracted tuberculosis.

Our lungs were being populated with old clothes and panting excavators.

During those years I made the Quixotic decision

to be a writer

in Spain

while renouncing neither my independence nor my freedom.

An undertaking that would never succeed.

Through these twenty years writing... I've never been able to be a writer in my own country.

And I'm just one example among many!

Your government, and your censors, who had rotted my lungs, who had robbed me of my father

kept me from the thing I had more right to than the tree has to the soil:

writing in my own language.

Anyone who wants to write has no choice but to either capitulate

or fight heroically, risking life or liberty every day or flee.

Like Saint Theresa of Ávila, how many of us left Spain to conquer glory.

Like so many hundreds of thousands of emigrants.

* * *

For years your national-syndicalist fanatics—amid shouts of "Viva la Revolución"—were always proclaiming that we must do away with art, the instrument of the "democratic-anarcho-Marxist-liberal conspiracy."

This memory provides a bonus stimulant for writers to exercise the profession.

And, since it's a profession as worthy as any other,

without giving it special importance and without neglecting it either,

I want to explain to you how a writer who above all wants to remain incorruptible lives in today's Spain

The free artist or writer doesn't "exist" for your followers

When someone, in an interview, mentions the name of one of them—censorship draws a line through it,

in any list of writers "et cetera" will be substituted for this name

those who might cite the name on radio or TV are informed that the broadcast will be interrupted, ipso facto, if this occurs

They don't exist.

Or rather, they do exist, when it's a matter of defaming them

Their works will be censored, prohibited

The insults will follow them and they won't be

able to defend themselves or protest

The person best informed about the repercussions of the independent writer's work abroad is, in fact, the Minister of Information:

A vast dossier on the writer, with clippings from around the world, will be dedicated to him

Clippings that are used against him.

Because in Spain, today, the authorities not only provide no support for the incorruptible artist, they are on the alert,

taking notes,

calling all the embassies,

in order to better attack him.

Artists, among others, like Cervantes, Velazquez, Picasso.

And so your worms advance, mowing down the future—uprooting light, music, color, the word—wiping it out like a plague of locusts.

* * *

During my visit to Madrid—1967—your "justice" imprisoned me.[23]

---

[23] The arrest was for writing an obscene, anti-patriotic and blasphemous (and no doubt, in jest) inscription on a book. Complete accounts are available, among other places, in the New

This earned me some contact with the current penitentiary realities.

It may surprise you when I tell you what made me most indignant: that minor delinquents are tortured fairly systematically in police stations.

Why?

Bureaucratic efficiency.

A police chief, having received a certain number of crime reports, tries to charge the first person he can with all the crimes.

There's a system for that: torture.

If it happens this method doesn't work with the really professional delinquents, those who resist under hours and days of torture, it works quite well with neophytes, for example car thieves.

So many of the latter rack up decades of jail sentences for having stolen one car, a crime augmented by a whole series of imaginary crimes they confess to under torture.

Those kids at the Carabanchel reform school, cast in the role of bandits because their sentences

---

York Times, starting July 25, 1967. Attending the trial—or writing— in support were Ionesco, Cela, Beckett, Anouilh, Mauriac, Rostand and others. An acquittal followed, after the summer months in jail.

were 80, 120, 140 years, when in reality their sole crime was stealing a car to go for a spin with their girlfriend.

The tortures political prisoners are systematically subjected to can eventually come to light… but—the common prisoners? Who will remember them?

So many friends, wounded, tortured!

regular people, also political types,

like my fellow student in law school who nearly lost his sight under interrogation,

like that pilferer at Carabanchel—for his whole life his face will show the marks from the punches, and the famous ring, of a Madrid police chief.

Men with eyes of rubber, Erector Set hearts and scrap-iron hands distribute martyrdom in your name: Pity our Spanish petty thieves!

The atmosphere of hypocrisy that reigns in the country's jails has been institutionalized.

The prisons are
administered
surveilled
by a third of their own prisoners
who are called "destinos."

Their job is to squeal on the others.

Their mission is to inform, spy on and torment the prisoners, their companions.

The most soulless of the "destinos" are in charge of the punishment cells, and often sadistically brutalize the poor men who, like rats, spend days, weeks, months between the four walls.

The strongest "destinos" attack those who try to escape; beatings end with wounds or deformities.

I've known so many prisoners who have stayed for six months (some for a year) locked day and night in underground punishment cells:

unable to

read,

write,

smoke,

receive visits,

or talk to anyone.

During these long months the life of the prisoner buried alive proceeds in a tiny pen, in darkness and silence, with no way of knowing if it is day or night, with only the hope of a cockroach with whom to whisper a bit.

These men emerge half blind and half crazy, so

much so that when their punishment ends they can't rejoin the ordinary cells but instead a unit called PISTA, where, little by little, they regain their vision and mental balance.

I'm telling you something that's going on, right now, in every Spanish prison.

What can anyone do, in the midst of this silence, the general "Amen"? So much pain is locked in these Spanish jails, at Burgos, at Carabanchel, at El Peñon del Hacho. Just writing the names of these prisons makes me tremble.

When I got out of jail I wrote a letter, in the Paris paper *Le Monde*, which nobody in Spain could have published:

..."I have known of a certain number of cases which I could not keep quiet without being ashamed of myself:

—a thirty-year-old floor cleaner sentenced in 1966 to 13 years for association and illegal propaganda

—one of his comrades accused of the same crimes got 15 years

—a bullfighter was sentenced to 6 years in jail for 'insult to the nation' because, in his anger after a traffic accident, he said 'Spanish people are jerks'

—after 20 years of detention a worker was finally set free; in 1947 he had tried to organize a union

—a progressive student who was carrying 9 copies of a leftist magazine was condemned to 3 years in jail

—a Madrid intellectual was sentenced to 12 years for having written 2 articles in a foreign newspaper,"

etc.

at the end of this letter I was saying

"I belong to nothing and nobody. I only want freedom to prevail, and that injustice no longer crushes us all. I would like to be able to believe that everything I have just exposed is false,

that I was wrong,

that what I saw and lived in Spain this summer was only a nightmare."

What I was expressing was that I would have been glad to be wrong

I still had a faint hope that, with facts in hand, it would be shown that my eyes and ears had deceived me.

When I learned that the Spanish Embassy was

replying to me, I had a certain satisfaction

How great was my disappointment when I read the words of a miscellaneous advisor (of I don't know what)

readers were informed that, contrary to what had been said, some functionary or other of the Information Ministry had played no role in my incarceration.

But, about my serious accusations—NOTHING! So they were accurate.

* * *

And my Paris letter was restrained.

I could have added the case

of a Spanish poet 17 years old

arrested, I repeat, at the age of 17

and who spent 24 (twenty-four) years of his life in prison after his arrest

On leaving the jail his eyesight, accustomed to never gazing at the horizon but only the four walls of his cell, was extraordinarily traumatized.

This youngest of poets, 17 years old, had to wait until the age of 41 (after 24 years in jail) to make love to a woman for the first time

Your men buried his male sex and male heart under mud, for ages

Tell me, what horrible crimes did he commit?

For a crime of opinion

for loving a different kind of Spain

for a burning idealism

a man, like so many others, spent his entire youth in jail.

The metal worker, Melquésidez Rodriguez-Chao, wrote his own testimony, one full of hope and showing no bitterness at all, a book I recommend to you.

The title itself howls:

24 Years In Prison

(he was 20 when his captivity began)

He writes, for example:

"The Penitentiary at Burgos is legendary. Truly horrendous crimes have been committed there... You can still see the patches in the walls looking over the Patio of the Acacias, spots from which the machine guns were aimed, mowing down antifrancoists *en masse*. Thousands of men have died in that prison, or left it with one foot in the grave... Innumerable, the sufferings inflicted there."

* * *

I'm going to tell you something sad: your Spain of today

not only took away my health, my father, my language

but often takes away my friends

How many of them, after a campaign against me, stop seeing me or writing to me, to steer clear of any difficulties?

Who could throw the first stone at them?

Your regime is to blame

Yet once in a while missives flutter in to me, from the heart

I have just received a letter from a Spanish man I don't know, who tells me his father might have been with mine in Peñon del Hacho prison

He tells me

"There are differences between our two cases

My father was shot without any kind of a hearing

But they had the delicacy to notify him beforehand so that 'he could get right with God.'

I have here his farewell letter, which was

smuggled to us;

my mother died of grief two months later; she had lost 66 pounds.

Our reticence was such that we have never spoken of my father.

My feelings toward him are complicated: it is as if I had killed him

and I am dragging his corpse

as the convict in French Guyana dragged his ball and chain."

How many of us have a ball and chain like that.

* * *

The entire country forced to hold back what their souls are shouting

They are all enemies of your regime

everything threatens your system:

from a simple theater play to a meeting among three workers

from a pamphlet to a banner

Is this possible?

Hurtling in your terror, locked in your palace, you live the nightmare of the Black Legend and impose it on every Spaniard

Is it possible, that anyone could want this kind of Spain?

Could there be some motivation that escapes me?

some supreme explanation?

We are many—we Spaniards who, like me, would like someone to explain to us,

who want to understand.

But we're convinced there is nothing to understand

It is time to give all Spaniards the chance to elect the system of governance they prefer.

Spain should welcome everyone,

we have to end the discrimination that began centuries ago.

A microscopic example, among many:

My daughter who—rejected by our Embassy in Paris, where I was trying to register her—

does not have the right to be my daughter: because her parents didn't get married in strict adherence to your religious dogmas. For your government, I—married for fifteen years—am single; and my daughter is a bastard.

When will your Spain stop "putting handcuffs

on the flowers"?[24]

* * *

So much hate!

I don't want, nor do any of us, to know anything about this Spain of which you are inheritor and representative. A Spain whose sovereigns lay dying amid mental defectives and storks with their throats slit. Palaces and Courts pleased, for centuries, to live among dwarfs, monsters, idiots, and ass-kissers: your "men of pleasure" (sic), in order to better tyrannize the people. Funereal Courts in which every day an elephant climbed the narrow stairs to the third floor of the Escorial to keep Philip II's son company during breakfast.

While the people exploded in the clandestine "burying of the sardine" festival (the men dressed as women, women as men, kids disguised as old people and old ladies as cats in heat), at the same time swearing to do away with religious authority and its Lents, in the midst of Dionysian celebration

And the Inquisitors imposed intolerance, torture, blood and hatred just like today. Only in Spain are

---

24 *Y Pusieron Esposas a las flores* (with some variations in the title) is one of Arrabal's best known plays.

the Carabanchel prison or burning-at-the stake in Seville, Torquemada or the assassination of Grimau not anachronisms.

Your Spain reeks. This Spain of "Viva la Muerte" that sullies all things.

What horror I feel, thinking of you sleeping every night next to the perfectly preserved arm of Saint Theresa of Ávila, that fascinating woman the Inquisition persecuted so willfully and whom your people would have martyred if she were among us today.

* * *

I'm going to copy a smuggled letter for you, from a man condemned to death by your followers and who had no "subversive" ideas beyond a simple philanthropy.

Your "justice" not only took his life but also kept him from communicating with his wife and children before he died.

This letter (so innocent and therefore exemplary) miraculously reached his loved ones.

It says:

> Dear Flora and dear children,

I hope the present moment finds you well, I'm alright for now.

Shortly I'm being taken from the jail to an end that is tragic for me and at the same time for you and my beloved children. You all know well the way I have always tried to do right, for everyone in general. I hope all your lives may come to their ends less tragically than mine, and that you always keep good will, no matter the ill reward. As for me, I will hold steady in my sense of justice and human equity to the very end.

For my children I only hope they keep the goodness they now show, that they carry on bravely and well, and that they have rancor for no one and don't avenge my death. Be good, my children, toward your mother, and try to be as useful as possible for society. Perhaps you will experience a better society, one with better human feeling—help to perfect it. Always nurture and maintain a good conscience and you will be happy even when luck is bad—know that no one can distort your good actions.

My children, your father will die within a few hours. I see death coming and believe me, I am calm. I love you all so much that I go off leaving you a kiss that springs from the bottom of my heart.

And to you dear Flora, my lasting embrace. I bear you engraved in my heart and nobody can tear you away. You can be sure that when the finger pulls the trigger I will be giving you a last kiss. You can be at peace—your Macario will know how to die as he has lived.

To all of you I send a kiss with my last breath.

—Macario

In the margin of this letter a cell mate has written:

When Macario heard his name called by the executioner he bit down on my arm—hard.

* * *

How long will Spain have to bite the arm of a friend, in order to keep its suffering silent?

Without bitterness. Sincerely.

Arrabal
Paris, March 18, 1971.

Epilogue

(by Francisco González Viera, from the original 1972 edition)

Spanish censorship has prevented the publication of Arrabal's plays in his own language... Worse still, a Madrid publisher (TAURUS, in the collection PRIMER ACTO) has assembled three short plays written fourteen years ago under the heading "Arrabal's Theater"; the plays are so heavily abridged that you can't tell what is going on. One of the plays even shows up with a false title: *Guernica*[25] was changed to *Ciugrena*. The little book inevitably gives a false impression of its author. Naturally Arrabal can do nothing to take this deformity out of circulation... such is the collusion of publisher, judicial system and the authorities in today's Spain.

Christian Bourgois Editions (Paris) is about to publish Arrabal's complete works in Spanish. The first volume of plays (Theater I) has already appeared.

---

25 By the time of this title-change, Picasso's painting *Guernica* had steadily increased world outrage at Franco's invitation to Hitler to bomb the Basque village of that name.

When, in 1969, the Núria Espert company tried for the first and only time to stage one of the author's plays ("The Two Executioners" ... a play twenty minutes long) the theater was occupied by armed police, the posters shredded, and the playbills destroyed.

Thus the paradox: now that Arrabal is published and staged everywhere in the world he cannot see either his books or his plays in his own country. The greatest living Spanish dramaturge... does not exist for Spaniards, by government decree.

Arrabal has said: "I have as much right to write in Spanish as a tree has to the soil." This is not the opinion of those who rule the country. The co-founder of the Falange declared in *Arriba*, the newspaper of the official (and only) party, that Arrabal should be castrated "*so that—incapable of being a father—he would not produce children who would renounce the Country.*"

Coda: Lullabies of the Onion

(by Miguel Hernández, written from Franco's prison after the war in response to a letter from his wife saying there was nothing to eat but bread and onions. The poet died in prison in 1942.)

An onion is frost
hunkered and poor
The frost of your days
and my nights.
Hunger and onion,
black ice and deep
hugging frost.

> My boy lay
> in hunger's cradle.
> Onion blood
> to suckle.
> But your blood
> was frosted with sugar,
> onion and hunger.
> A dark-haired woman,
> resolute with moon,
> spills thread upon thread
> over the cradle.
> Laugh, son,

and swallow the moon
when the time comes.
Lark of my household,
laugh often.
The laugh in your eyes
is the light of the world.
Laugh so much
that, hearing you,
more space will beat in men's souls.
Your laugh sets me free,
gives me wings.
Chases my solitude,
dashes the cell walls.
Your mouth is soaring,
and your heart on those lips
is lightning.

Your laugh is the sword
victorious,
conqueror of flower
and lark.
The sun's rival.
Future of my bones
and of my love.

A fluttering of flesh,
and rapid eyelid,
the child blushing
as never before.
How many finches
flutter, and climb,
from your body!
I wakened out of childhood:
don't you awake.
I wear my mouth sadly:
laugh forever.
Still in your cradle,
defending laughter
feather by feather.
So high your flight,
so sprawling,
that your flesh is a sky
new born.
If only I could climb
to the source
of your soaring!

> In your eighth month you laugh
> with five orange blossoms.

With five tiny
ferocities.
With five teeth
like five jasmine flowers
still growing.
They will be the frontier
of tomorrow's kisses,
when you feel your tooth
as weapon.
When you feel fire
sinking in your teeth,
seeking the center.
Fly, son, in the double
moon of the breast:
it, onion-sad;
you, now sated.
Don't fall apart.
Never know the state of things
nor what is going on.

DIÁLOGOS
NEW ORLEANS
DIALOGOSBOOKS.COM

www.ingramcontent.com/pod-product-compliance
Lightning Source LLC
Chambersburg PA
CBHW032332110426
42744CB00036B/233